# Honey in the Vein

# Honey in the Vein

### E.D. Watson

Bric-a-Brac

Press

Bric-a-Brac Press

Copyright © 2023 E.D. Watson

Cover illustration: Rebecca Bowman

Book design: Rebecca Bowman

All rights reserved

ISBN: 9781961136021

# Author's Note

If you've never heard of St. Mary of Egypt, you aren't alone. An obscure saint venerated mostly by Catholics and Eastern Christians, she's often depicted as a naked, wild-looking desert dweller, with shaggy white hair and protruding ribs. Which is to say, not the sort of pretty lady saint made into garden statuary. She is thought to have lived some time between the fourth and fifth centuries, C.E., if she lived at all. There is no proof of her existence, only oral tradition passed from monk to monk, until one of them decided to write it down.

According to tradition, Mary left home at a young age, and became a sex worker in Alexandria during the time when Constantine's Christianity was sweeping the Roman Empire. In some versions of the story, she isn't a sex worker, she was just a nasty woman who really liked sex and had a lot of it, with men who aren't her husband. The OG party girl, Mary also liked rich food, wine, and bawdy songs. Around the age of thirty, she joined a group of pilgrims on their way to Jerusalem, ostensibly to party with them. According to the tale, she behaved so scandalously on the journey that even she's surprised the sea didn't swallow her.

Upon arrival in Jerusalem, she is swept along with the crowd toward a shrine housing a relic of Christ's cross, but an "unseen force" prohibits her from entering the church. She retreats to the side of the cathedral in shame, where she has a mystical experience. In a vision, Mary the Mother of Jesus tells Mary of Egypt to cross the Jordan River and go into the desert.

Mary does as she's told and spends the next forty years of her life as a hermit, praying and levitating. The only reason we know of her existence is because a monk named Zosimas is supposed to have found her during his own Lenten retreat into the wilderness.

Traditionally, Mary of Egypt is venerated during Holy Week, as a penitent. But women (and everyone else) have enough stories designed to reinforce restrictive gender norms and control behavior through shame. We've cast stones at each other, called each other names, and burned each other at the stake. It's time to stop.

This is Mary of Egypt's story then, reimagined. While I have taken certain liberties by reinterpreting some events and filling in lacunae in the tale, the major touchstones of her story remain intact.

E. D. Watson

*for all the Marys*

## Table of Contents

| | |
|---|---|
| In the Beginning | 1 |
| A Pretty Thing | 3 |
| Spinning | 5 |
| Rootbound | 7 |
| In Darkness | 9 |
| Brother's Keeper | 10 |
| Passage | 12 |
| Crescent City | 14 |
| Sekhmet | 16 |
| Body | 19 |
| I Know You Are, But What Am I? | 20 |
| Quid Pro Quo | 22 |
| Crone | 24 |
| Sekhmet II | 26 |
| Insatiable | 28 |

| | |
|---|---|
| Wine | 30 |
| Hoopoe | 32 |
| Last Bloom | 34 |
| Pilgrims | 36 |
| Passage II | 38 |
| Via Dolorosa | 39 |
| Harrowing | 40 |
| Jerusalem at Dawn | 42 |
| Vision | 44 |
| Olive Tree | 46 |
| Prayer | 51 |
| The First Day | 53 |
| Wilderness | 54 |
| Sparrows | 56 |
| Caravan | 58 |
| Honey in the Vein | 60 |
| Paradise | 62 |

| | |
|---|---|
| Sand | 63 |
| Forsaking the Gaze | 65 |
| The Monk | 67 |
| They Say | 69 |
| I Am | 72 |
| Communicant | 73 |
| Rain | 75 |
| | |
| Acknowledgments | 79 |

# PART I

# In the Beginning

Before breath ever filled my lungs,
when I was yet a clot of blood
with gills, a tail, and blackblind eyes,
I had the longings of a whale:
Leviathan inside of the
dark fishbowl of my mother's womb.
She must have felt a certain dread,
for why else go in secret to
a soothsayer, who for two coins
pronounced her sinking feelings true:
that I was not another son.
Two boys had she already, but
to please my father, Mother hoped
to spare him the collateral.
The soothsayer just shook her head
and gave my mother more bad news:
I was a woman fully formed;
my heart already had its teeth.
This one will run and cut her feet

upon the road, and marry not,

nor give thee anything but grief.

But take no bitter herb in tea

for she will see the face of God

in her own time and her own way.

# A Pretty Thing

At ten years old I understood
men looked at me more than they should.
Like a pull-toy on a string
I drew their gazes after me
in the streets and at the market.

The fruit man gave me extra dates,
the basket weaver offered dolls
of braided straw, a pretty thing
for a pretty thing, he whispered
and smiled with his rotted teeth.

My mother took the gifts away
and gave them to my brothers,
allowing me no pleasure
in what my honor had not earned.

Society's respect, she said,
is a woman's greatest treasure,

so walk as though invisible,

pretend your face is marred by pox.

Toss not your hair as though a beast

lest you be yoked to shame, a weight

too heavy for your back to bear.

But I believed another creed:

that being ugly was a sin,

the only unforgivable.

And deep within my homespun robes

my beauty smoldered like a coal

for me to set the world on fire;

I thought it was my soul.

# Spinning

Each day my mother spun her flax;
between her fingers narrow cord
from distaff unto spindle passed,
dust-colored thread, a narrow path
like those which scarred the shepherds' hills
beyond the borders of our town.

And while she spun she spoke to me
of goddesses Egypt once loved,
called pagan now by Constantine.
An ugly word, my mother said,
for hips that spread to make the world.
And now, she said, we worship He
who has the manner of a man,
our magic driven underground,
misunderstood and oft-maligned.

The spindle swung below her knee,
a pendulum that we could ask

the future of: Will I be rich?
Will Father bring fresh fish to us?
Will all the white cat's kittens live?
We played this game for hours on end
but ultimately failed to see
how closed the future was to me.
For soon my woman's blood arrived;
she gave me spindle of my own.

Said she: A woman's heart finds peace
in ceaseless movement of her hands.
And if bad luck should widow you,
you shall not starve, but can earn bread.
Outsized desires burred my flax
but it would never do to ask
what more the world might have for me,
for like the spindle I was meant
to be bound up, and occupied.

# Rootbound

I saw my brothers down below,
playing in the street. But I was
a woman now, locked up within
the cooking smells and heaps of thread,
and Mother caught me at the sill
too often for propriety.

She bid me tend her potted plants
behind the screens in old clay jars.
Such wilderness was I allowed,
contained, confined, a tiny land,
a minute portion of the world.

For marjoram and mint I grieved,
in each clay jar a jar-shaped ache
spread from the center to the edge
of where each root was limited.
Each day was passed just like the next,
a bit of sun, a bit of shade,

intended for domestic use,

no threat of ever growing large,

no trees were these, but simple herbs

for men to eat, to be consumed

by mortal mouths, not holy flames.

# In Darkness

I saw my brothers at their books;
I listened as they read the poems
in Greek, learned to count, to be men,
a thing I longed to also be.

Mother pulled me from the carpet
where I listened too intently
and gave to me another chore.

Then Second Brother came to me
and offered me a chance to learn
the words in secret, after dark.

A trade, he whispered, mine for yours.
Though indecent, I consented
and so he came into my room
and relieved me of my ignorance.

# Brother's Keeper

Brother darling when they caught us
who was I to you? A sister
who would one day be forgotten?

When Father wrenched your arm, you said
(like Adam had once said of Eve),
It was her fault, she told me to!

You had no birthright but possessed
position in our father's house,
the smallest rights unknown to me,

the right to go outside and play,
the right to speak and choose a trade,
but if we suffered poverty

the final spoonful of the meat
was given to our eldest brother;
we ate last, and ate the least.

Our father said you'd spoiled me;
that very night I left our home
already knowing where I'd go

for I could read a poem, a map,
the posted times for sailing ships.
I saved my life because of you.

# Passage

I paid my fare to board a boat
with money taken from the jar
where Mother kept her market coins.

I paid another woman too,
who waited on the dock with me:
two coins and she would call me hers
while we sailed, protecting me.

The woman gladly took my coins
but asked me not my name nor why
a child might flee, sparing me a lie.

I heard the water slap the hull
a thousand times for insolence.
The woman did not speak to me
nor share with me her loaf of bread.

I cowered near her hungrily
and laid my face against her thigh;
she pushed me from her with her knee.
The men on board saw all of it.

How easily a friendless girl
might disappear into the sea.

# Crescent City

O, city at the river's mouth,
she takes me in and sings to me
the song that promises to all
a welcome there within her gates.

Child, come, she says, belong to me.
Here, soul and body closely knit,
where monks pass prostitutes on streets,
arrayed like trays of fruit and meat.

If God is love, they tell the monks,
then come love me, come give me God.
The monks pretend they do not hear
the invite ringing in their loins.

At night I sleep beneath the docks
inhaling cast-net creatures' smells:
the spiny urchins no one wants
and fish heads tossed for cats to eat.

It all belongs and is all blessed:
the lamp smoke and the mugs of wine,
the sailors' songs and angel choirs,
the frankincense and burning dung,

the whine of the snake charmer's horn
and unfamiliar words like spells
enchant me and I fall in love
with wondrous Alexandria.

# Sekhmet

At noon from sleep my lady wakes
and bids me bring her tea and cakes.
They know her name across the sea

and call my lady Lioness,
for what she wants, my lady takes
the same way she selected me,

plucked from the trash upon the streets.
Most beautiful of women, she,
her gates a site of pilgrimage

for men who come at night in need,
the gifts they bear fit for a queen:
the finest kohl to line her eyes

and hammered silver for her wrists,
cups inlaid with precious jewels,
embroidered silk and casks of wine.

For nothing Sekhmet wants but time
to entertain them all: each night
she chooses one or two, each night

a teeming throng is turned away,
their offerings left with calling cards
and poems that Sekhmet cannot read.

The ways by which she chooses them
my lady slowly teaches me.
I am her student and her toy,

a ploy by which she lures them in,
for I am only just thirteen.
Live for yourself, she says to me,

for what else are our bodies made
but wine and dance and acts of love?
What misery is piety!

Girl, take a lover, take a drink,
take necklaces, and baths in milk.
For at your tender age, says she,

a girl can ask for anything.
Bless the fire from which we're made,
exploit them for their base desires;

pretend each night that you are pure.
She pinches me on my behind
and says by rights the world is mine.

# Body

I am a fatted calf; how sleek
my thighs and rounded belly,
my breasts like fruit, my thighs like yams—
I know how to smile halfway,
to halfway close my amber eyes.
I could bewitch a god this way;
with men I hardly need to try.
The flush upon my throat, and how
it flutters when I drink my wine—
O, I am wondrous beautiful
in this abundant flesh of mine!
My treasure, faithful friend, my pet.
In all creation, I love it best.

# I Know You Are, But What Am I?

Why must I be a good girl? Why
can't I be a freak? What's wrong with
wanting pleasure? What is so wrong
with wanting sleep? My poor mother
arose each dawn before the sun
and did my father ever thank her?
Did he even see? Everything
we did was done to please him
and then to please the little lords,
my brothers. But let me ask you,
and let yourself say honestly
why a woman should feel nothing
but devotion? Why should she be
hungry all her life for life? Please.
Since I was a child I have nursed
an appetite for more than bread;
I want meat, every single night
and I want the men who bring it
with perfume on their beards and chests.

I want them at my feet, singing,

reciting poems like scripture, verse

after verse, reversal of things—

let them be the ones to bring me

groceries, flowers. Pay my light bill.

They say the body is a temple;

come worship at my altar then.

## Quid Pro Quo

Outside, men are digging a trench
for blood and piss and rain to flow
between the buildings and the street.
What the city excretes will run
by my doorstep: a stinking creek
to stain my robes and draw the flies.

They have the bodies of young gods,
toiling, hairless bronze and sweating
beneath the bright sun of midday.
All morning I watch them work
and listen at my window to
their banter. You know who lives here,
one of them says to the others.

The young man grins and starts to sing
a love song, softly, near my screen
a song called The Hoopoe, for its
mournful cry. Come home, little bird,

for your parents are dying, come
back to the one who has loved you,
return to the one who has cried.

And beware, I sing back to him,
for love is but a pretty trap,
a snare, a boy with a string.
The young god smiles. Come in, I say.
Let me offer you something cool
to drink. Come wash your face and neck.
Tell me your name. Let us mingle
our voices in another song.

He says he'd like that very much.
Build me a bridge, sweetheart, I say,
so that you may come over here
without tracking filth on my rugs,
where you may lie and take some rest.
Build me a little bridge and then
come inside. Bring your handsome friend.

# Crone

I felt it leap inside my womb,
a twitch of rotten luck, I'm done,

this can't be happening. And yet
each day my blood fails to arrive.

My lady slaps my face three times.
Now everyone will know, she says,

she says I've ruined everything.
Not me, I think. Not me but them.

Go see the woman at the end
of the street, take these coins she says.

Without speaking the old woman
reaches under my tunic, looks

into my eyes and gives to me
a packet of foul-smelling herbs.

Not all women make good mothers.
Not all women want the same things.

Praise be to women, women's ways—
praise be to clinics and nurses,

praise to midwives burned as witches,
the pharmacists and herbalists

all keeping disaster at bay—
surely this is goodness and mercy.

## Sekhmet II

My mistress languishes near death.
None of her lovers come to her

to say goodbye, or to recall
those tender passions she once stoked.

Where are they who love me best?
she cries to me from her stained bed.

The smell of sickness choking me,
I feed her watered wine and broth,

but in my heart I scorn her pain,
her woman's weakness now laid bare:

that she had somehow needed them,
that after all they were not prey,

that they could hurt her, even now.
And she is hideous to me

whom I once loved and was lovely.
She has become a bridge of bones.

# Insatiable

I do not love the men, but how
they clasp me to their chests and stroke
my back. I love to rest there in the small
oblivions that follow our
ascent. I love their hands stilled in
my hair, their faces at my breasts.
Eros is a red-plumed bird,
its song will fill a thousand sails,
but seldom do those boats go far;
such birds live but the briefest lives,
unlike the hoopoe, who returns.
Men can only imitate love—
learned caresses from their mothers,
with gentle words and lullabies—
I let them pet me like a child,
forgetting how like children they
arrived, a-tremble with such need
that in those moments I could ask
for them to give me anything:

a pouch of gold, a lemon tree,
another man's head, on a plate.
They call me names they do not mean:
their Apricot, their Little Bird,
pretty words like songs that fade when
the flute is lowered from the lips.
What names they call me, that I am:
a Temptress, Goddess, Virgin, Prize—
but Monster suits me best of all,
body with a mouth at both ends,
who hungers and cannot be fed.
They have no milk to offer me;
I try to take their souls instead,
and suck the marrow from their bones,
the color from their simple lives,
and toss them, emptied, from my sill
back to their homes
      and babes
          and wives.

# Wine

My true love is a goblet gold,
into which the red wine flows.

My true love is a crude clay cup,
dark drink trembling at its brim.

My true love is my own hand dipped
into the cask, the drops like blood

spotting the tile and my chin.
Wine to gladden the hearts of men,

oil to make their faces shine,
the Psalmist called these things a gift

from the one who sees and knows hearts
are not glad; joy no natural state.

Consider it like medicine.
It helps me live, remakes my hands

as hands again instead of claws,
returning me unto myself

in a form that I can bear:
my dark reflection wavering

in the center of the cup,
a woman I can swallow.

# Hoopoe

The stories that we tell ourselves
about ourselves, the what and why
of who we have been, who we are,
are but a way that we survive
inside the wet wool of our lives.
We crave illusion of a tide,
some forward motion, some design,
so we call ourselves the heroes.

My family has forgotten me,
but O if they could see me now!
The finest oil, the sweetest wine
brought to me by those who want me—
see how I have become adored!

See how I shed my reputation,
worthless encumbrance that it was.
Little good it did my mother,
who could not read nor choose her life,

whereas I freely move about,
iconoclast and modern triumph—
this is what I tell myself.

But the hoopoe that each dawn comes
to my window like a ghost-bird
sings out a bitter song to me:
*Your mother died alone*, it cries.
Be gone, I say.
Away it flies.

## Last Bloom

Alexandria is played out.
Now fewer young men come to me;
my lovers like old husbands lie,
the years in bags beneath their eyes,
their noses red, their faces wrinkled:
last year's dates upon my pillow.
They come to me to pass the time
and to remember who they were
when I knew them in their prime.
They say I am still beautiful,
no threads of silver at my brow,
though time has left its thumbprints near
the outer corners of my eyes.
They tell me I am like fine wine:
better now that I am older.
What have we but threadbare stories
that make my soles itch, like the rug
worn thin by too much foot traffic?
Oh, to shut my door forever,

to no more let them in to me—
I refill their glasses, longing
to escape the thing between us,
dead lust like wine turned vinegar.
If I say: I do not love you,
I love the way you made me feel
once upon a long lost time,
when I ruled the world through you—
I miss the power I once had,
they remind me that they raised me.
They watched my hips swell like the dunes,
and have known me half my lifetime.
I sometimes do not charge these men
for my diminished company,
relying on my other trade.
I sit and silently make thread,
though I despise the lonely hours
spinning flax without a daughter.
I do not ask the spindle of
my future, for I know it: lost.

# Pilgrims

The white-winged creatures overhead
are seagulls and not angel guides,

birds greedy as the men who swarm
beneath them on the dock, arrived

in new robes clad, clasping bundles:
pilgrims, for Jerusalem bound.

Brothers, brothers, take me with you,
I call to them and flash my smile.

Pay my fare and I will bless you;
I swear I will be worth your while.

A pilgrimage is perilous
and each man thinks that he could die.

Each wants the comfort of a breast
to lay his head on, like a babe.

They consent to take me with them,
the milk-lust tickling each one's throat.

## Passage II

There is no room up on the deck
where all the sunlight and fresh air
belong exclusively to men,
of whom several paid my fare.
I promised them to be worthwhile
and now I wait here in the hold
among the freight and sloshing bilge.
They visit me like a latrine
sans ceremony or desire
for these are men who hate their need
and call me Mary Magdalene,
the whore who followed after Christ.
Then, having finished, turn their backs
and go back up into the light.

# Via Dolorosa

The crowd's momentum carries me
amid a throng of unwashed men.

These pilgrims are the very ones
who pressed their bodies into mine

now inflamed with love for God,
a glassy-eyed mob, chanting psalms.

I see this as a kind of joke,
but no one joins me in my laughter.

To the church, I cry, to the church!
O, let us push the whole thing over!

# Harrowing

What arms are these that keep me out?
God stationed angels at the door.

It makes me hate Him all the more
that these men should be forgiven,

these loathsome ones He will allow
to kiss a fragment of the cross

when I have kissed those blistered mouths!
But they are men and that is why

all their failings are permitted,
while my entrance is forbidden—

I jab my elbows in their ribs
and slide my shoulders into gaps,

and yet each time I reach the door
an unseen force then pushes back.

Seven times this force repels me
before my hate becomes a grief

and I stumble towards the garden
enraged but sapped of all my strength.

# Jerusalem at Dawn

The stalls are shuttered in the gloom,
trash heaped in corners of the street
where stones in shadow kiss and grind
just as they've done for centuries.
Morning prayers are dashed from windows
like washwater into the street
and yet you slumber, still dreaming.

In the blue time of your sleepworld
God walks the shadowed alleyways
among the lean and yellow-eyed
cats of the holy land, gnawing
stale bread crusts dropped by pilgrim hands.

Our Lord simmers. Our Lord is not
a man. God is not an icon.
God doesn't live inside a church;
God lives on the street. God's hungry.
God is the empty blue feeling

before lunging at a rat.

God is sandfooted and wildeyed

and God's favorite times are twilight

and just before dawn. The blue time.

The time when you are still, asleep.

# Vision

What is this light that shines on me?
I am struck blind, and only see
her feet, which glide like slender boats
above the roots and paving stones:
Mother Mary, with Sekhmet's face.
Her hands resolve as she moves in,
her fingers shedding beams of light.
She speaks and it sounds like the tide:

What you despise is but illusion
collective built, collective held.
You stand outside the Kingdom gates,
you who've searched the hinterlands,
God is your breath, the in and out.
Each day, a thousand times you say
God's only name without thinking.
So child cease your search for God
and learn the searcher's name instead.

Cross the river, to the desert.

You will find yourself there waiting.

Cross the river, enter the gates!

Everything you ever wanted

exists, but cannot be grasped—

though It may settle in your hands.

## Olive Tree

The birds begin to stir, I wake
beneath its branches like a beast.
I kiss the knuckles of its roots;
this tree may be the final one
beneath which I shall ever sleep.

I hang my necklace on a limb:
a parting gift from one who leaves
behind the world of greenery.
This gold was given for my soul,
a thing I sold and sold again.

A thing I now aim to recover,
like the pieces of a letter
tossed into the wind and scattered.
For I would like to read again
whatever once was written there,

to find the scraps of who I am
beyond this shade, where no one goes
except for madmen and for monks.
I turn my back now to the world.
If there be gods, then let them come.

# PART II

# Prayer

All I want is to stop wanting.

That I might stop these muttering
prayers that fleck my lips with foam.

That I grow still and let my lack
roll out like a carpet for god.

That I might stop expecting him.

That the sword should fall and split me
that the halves of me fall open

that my bones release the chorus
of greasy blackbirds nesting there,

that they may ascend, forgetting
     my name, that they may take my eyes
and ears so I no longer hear

      them gabbling about redemption.


That they may pick my body clean,
      devouring my lips which sang,
devouring my fingerprints.


That they may put their beaks into
the soft pulp of my heart, old fruit

      and carry it to god, an offering

      or rebuke.

# The First Day

Over one rise then another,
I walk and walk and walk toward
a distant, purple jagged ridge
of shadows like a ragged hem;

my kidskin slippers are in shreds.
Unfolding on my tongue, lotus
of thirst, saltflower, death-petaled.
My body longs to find a cave,

a shepherd's cave where I might stop
and eat a portion of my loaves;
there is no shade where I might rest,
and if I sit I might not stand.

And so I walk and walk and walk.

I will not turn back. I will not.

# Wilderness

O, out here, out here, out here is
nothing and I am nothing and
there is no Music, there is no
Mind. O, out here, out here, out here

I am lost and blest and nothing.
Is this freedom, Lord? Is this love?
O, what am I to make of You,
who were promised to me as One

Who Is and Always Is: Only.
I came out here believing,
what I can no longer recall.
Out here all there is, is silence.

Out here, there are no Myths, no Truths.
Or: all truth is myth. And what am I
to hold belief? A cracked vessel.
A loosely woven basket.

All that I might keep passes through.

# Sparrows

Inside me are a thousand voices,
a chorus of sparrows, restive,
each clamors for the seed
of my attention, which is scattered
haphazard and without aim.

A thousand sparrows are a burden,
heavier than you might think.
One cries out for a drink of wine
and swears to me that she will die.
One cries out for a roof and walls.

One remembers all my lovers
and sings their hands upon my hips.
Another one bemoans the loaves,
which harden in the desert air.
And still another voice recalls

that making thread was not so bad.
Across the empty plate of sky
scraps of memory scud and blow
like dust and leaves swept from a door:
the fruits that I once tasted,

sweet raisins and my brother's books.
All around me there's a silence
where nothing stirs and no one is.
I press myself against its walls
but cannot enter into it.

# Caravan

Across the silent desert dark
come sounds of jingling harness bells.
Men's voices singing far away
carry with their cooking smells.

Over one rise, then another
I keep inside the creeping cold
and think what I might offer them
for their spiced lentils and some wine.

I am no longer beautiful;
my skin is cracked, my hair gone white.
But they are men far from a town,
far from their wives and concubines;

such men desire to pass the time,
and though I might be called a crone,
I have much practice with abuse
and I can take it with some soup;

I watch their supper with desire
and fancy sucking on a bone—
my mouth grows wet to think of it.
From this group of camel drivers,

I watch one stand and walk away—
I search my mouth for words to say—
O, to be touched by human hands!
To hear a man's voice say my name!

I run and when I reach the pile
of rubble I call home, I weep
for there is nothing good it seems,
no joy I am allowed to keep.

This star-choked kingdom, no-man's land
is mine unto the blue horizon.
The landscape mirrors my own heart,
where longing has cut deep channels.

# Honey in the Vein

First: the pain is all that exists,
a scream between my bones and skin—
and then I open up my eyes.

Have I arrived in Hell at last?
The entrance of my cave is blue,
a promise of the coming sun.

Death did not, could not find me here.
Am I to live in agony
eternal as this empty land?

My ruined feet are sealed together
with blood gone dry and black as pitch,
my body brittle as a twig—

and how my weary muscles ache.
What difference can it now make
if I become a cannibal?

My sores reopen as I move;
I place my lips against my heel
to taste the wetness of my blood.

How thick it is! How strangely sweet.
Greedy, thirst-mad, I drink deeply
ouroboros, eating my tail.

The morning loses all its stars
and pales from indigo to gray.
I lift my face, I lift my face!

I dip my finger in the wound
and hold it up into the light
and gasp in wonder there to see

not blood but honey, dripping gold.

# Paradise

The desert tells me its secret:
it is a garden in disguise,
lush as any Eden, perfumed.

One has only to live here for
a while, for it to be transformed.
You think you know what beauty is?

You only know what you were taught:
long hair, big tits, a round backside.
They told you the desert was waste-

land, where men went mad from thirst, died.
Forbidding place. So you thought. But:
The sky is softer here than silk,

than any silk I ever wore.
It might look like I am naked,
but that is an illusion too.

# Sand

With each sunrise I am born;
each evening my life ends again
and I return to the in-between
where dreams unfold in me like blooms.

Come dawn their perfume lingers faint—
the scent of all that cannot be
learned in books or from a master,
but what is conveyed only to
a mind unfettered by assumption.

All I know is I know nothing.

I walk where I will, I suffer
and the suffering frees in me
a shape I never knew was there,
as wind will scallop a cliff-face.

Within each grain of sand, design.

Each one nothing but a fragment
of the stone from whence it has come:
the mountainside whose peak pierces
the clouds. Less than even this am I,

for nothing of me shall remain.
Each day there is less of me,
each day I come closer to myself.

Some day I shall scale a rise
and my village will be there.
I will go back and do it all
the same again, for how else could
I ever learn to really see
the sand for what it is? How else?

I scoop the sand into my palm
and marvel at the colors there:
the black and lavender and red.
To think these gems have always been
beneath my feet, beneath my bed.

## Forsaking the Gaze

My womanhood has always been
a kind of cloak, a mask I wear,
my eyes and limbs composed for men
who drink too much and call me names,
who call me darling daughter, whore.
Your hair, they say. We love your hair.
Such long hair! Your crowning virtue.

My father used to say to me,
Someday you'll drive your husband mad
by looking up at him that way.
How had I looked? I could not say.
I was a child, eating breakfast. But oh,
afterwards I practiced that look
in Mother's looking glass, chin tucked,
eyes peering up through my lashes.

Thus began my idolatry:
not of myself, no—of the men
casting furtive glances at me

from their market stalls, wives at hand,
or those who stared with frank desire—
I thought that I was powerful.
I thought that they would worship me,
but instead I worshiped them.

I thought I was my own mistress;
but all my life I was a slave
to their gazes, beheld in chains,
always theirs, theirs for the taking,
consumed like street food on the street.
And I don't want it anymore.
It's time I learned to love myself.

## The Monk

My brother has walked many miles
to find his way, and he's still lost.

    At first, he calls me a demon.
    Then we recognize each other,

fellow members of a family
who once sought God among the stones

    and in the promises of men,
    caught in a daily ritual

that only ever offered bread
which can feed, but never fill.

    We searched the world at separate ends
    to bring each other empty hands.

Thou art the sister of my soul,

he says, then kneels to kiss my feet

        black and hard as hooves they are now;
        the honey does not flow for him.

# They Say

They say Zosimas the monk found
me, that nude I ran away from
him, ashamed for him to see me.

They say he gave to me his cloak
to hide my withered breasts, my skin
burnt black. I did run, that part's true.

And true, I was nearly naked.
And true, I took his robe: habit
dies hard, and I was sometimes cold.

I never said I was a saint;
I was just a woman who dared
to satisfy my appetite

for knowledge, fine wine, love, a life.
I never said I was sorry.
He offered me some bread and wine;

they say that I accepted them.
Maybe. In the end we have to
give up everything we believe

even if it's nothing. Starving
or feasting: both are merely ways
of finding where the desert lies;

everyone has one in their soul.
It took me decades to arrive
at a place where I could let go

with gladness all that I had been
and live from star to star to star,
locust to honey, wind to wind.

But ask me if I am surprised
that this is what is said of me.
A woman without need of men

is in the end a threat to them.
They build a story like a cage,
some holy tale to keep her in.

# I Am

I am a spindle wrapped in thread,
a bone soaked in a bit of broth.

    I am a nameless no one, lost;
    I am a speck, numbered by God.

I am the sky spread overhead,
the falling stars that scratch its cheek.

    I am the furtiveness of flowers
    unblossoming within the sand.

I am the slender crescent of shade,
at the base of every stone.

    I am the freshet flowing clear,
    where birds and foxes come to drink.

I am neither man nor woman,
but something else, unbound and wild.

## Communicant

I am growing my old woman's face,
    becoming every day like mud

that dries and cracks beneath the glare.
    The cracks are where the dew gets in

and also how the dark escapes.
    I am a map. Find nowhere here.

My arms are two dry riverbeds,
    my legs wadis, waiting for rain.

These breasts once gently sloping hills
    changed to a pair of windblown dunes,

the ridge between them stepping stones
    from my heart to the hollow place.

I graze my fingers over them
    this landscape where I am pilgrim.

I search for souvenirs. What keeps?

I like myself better this way.

# Rain

In the distance, a sound unheard
for ages, yet known straightaway,

the thunder like hooves, my lover
arriving at my gate. He calls

and lightning splits the pewter sky
drawing behind it a veil of rain

to hide this union, dust made clay.
This is how demigods are made:

some woman like a patch of earth
catches the sky's eye and is taken.

The dry beds fill and churn,
gray stones are turned black again.

The sky empties into the sand.
A sigh, a silence follows, then

the frogs begin to chirr, cranes come
and slip their beaks into the streams.

The wedding feast goes on all night.
Stars rustle in the firmament like seeds—

O, paradise is everywhere

the garden is inside of me.

## Acknowledgments

Thank you to all poets everywhere, I love you. Thanks especially to the Wyrdd Writers, Cohort Number Three, and the crew at When the River Speaks. Thank you John, Cyra, Lisha, Alex.

Thank you to Rebecca at Bric-a-Brac for your vision, dedication, and general brilliance.

A whole pallet of yams for you, Kit.

Thank you Fr. Ben for encouraging me to write my way into the desert during Lent.

Thank you most of all to Jaime, my soulmate, camino buddy, and intergalactic partner in crime. May we always drink coffee together like this.

Bric-a-Brac
Press

www.ingramcontent.com/pod-product-compliance
Lightning Source LLC
Chambersburg PA
CBHW022122040426
42450CB00006B/803